All the Things I Couldn't Say

ALL THE THINGS
I Couldn't Say

MEGHAN LEIGH

by
ML

By Meghan Leigh
4017 Riley Fuzzel Rd.
STE 500 - P.O. Box 425
Spring, TX 77386

Published and printed in the United States of America.

First published by By Meghan Leigh, 2026

Cover design and illustration by Victoria Heath Silk
Book design and typesetting by InsideStudio26.com
Illustrations by Iulia Mirica
Edited by Martha Sprackland
Author Photo by Allison Ermon Photography

LCCN: 2025928026
ISBN: 979-8-9943862-0-0 (print) and 979-8-9943862-1-7 (e-book)

www.bymeghanleigh.com

For those who have struggled to articulate what they are experiencing in the way they wish they could. For those who have shattered over and over again, and who by some miracle have pieced themselves back together while remaining kind. For those who have done the hard work to find the beauty, purpose, and strength within. And for those still in the thick of it – I see you, and yes, you can. We are worthy, we are enough, we are whole.

Contents

The Origin — xi

Surviving — 3

Feeling — 19

Raging — 35

Learning — 51

Fighting — 67

Opening — 85

Hurting — 101

Asking — 117

Loving — 135

Grieving — 151

Crawling — 167

The Origin

journal entry, 2023

I'm really good with facts, with sharing things how they are with no emotions attached. This is how it started, this is what happened, and this is how it ended. And you know why? It's because I don't want people to worry about me. If I tell the story as if I'm fine, then it means I am fine… right? What a ginormous lie. I am not fine. I haven't been fine for a while, not by a long shot.

I stay busy to keep myself distracted, to make myself feel worthy, because I was taught that idle hands are lazy. Somewhere in my conditioning I tied my worth to what I can do, what I can provide to others, how I am thought of, and how I look. Growing up I was too tall, too broad, too quiet, too nice, too emotional, too much, and yet somehow not enough. Not good enough at sports, not smart enough, not tough enough, not outgoing enough, not enough like so and so, or like everyone else. So began my dance of walking the line between enough but not too much. Adapting to the whims and demands of others. Ever so slowly losing myself, as I became who and what I thought I was supposed to be, until I was just done.

Life had chewed me up, spit me out and come back for seconds. I didn't just break, I shattered like china. And here is the thing, I didn't want to be glued back together again. Because the pretty, perfect porcelain that broke wasn't actually me. It was the vessel that held me, the carefully painted ceramic exterior I had crafted. My true self was trapped inside, or maybe more accurately the makings of my true self were. It's been almost two years and I am still growing into a more whole version of myself. It's a challenge. Being yourself is as vulnerable as it is magical. So here goes my attempt at being vulnerable, honest and emotional while telling myself, and you, who I am.

I am Meghan. I am vibrant, radiant and grounded. I am fiercely loyal and protective of those I love. When my people need me I'm there, barriers be damned. I am light, I am laughter and I am deeply empathetic. I wear my heart on my sleeve, which is my strength and not my weakness. I will awaken every dragon, wolf and monster if someone tries to take advantage of me or mine. I have zero tolerance for bullies and idiots with a superiority complex and no humility. My greatest fear is being a disappointment to those I love. My brain moves at a million miles an hour and it's difficult to turn off most days; it's why I have a hard time being still and content. My mind is a vault: I remember a lot of things in great detail that others forget. I have a lot of patience for others and hardly any for myself. I hate when people forget me; it makes me sad, and I begin to question if I matter. I'm not sure if it says more about me or them. I'm in my mid-thirties and have no freaking clue what I'm doing with my life. I'm constantly torn between doing what I'm good at and wondering if I find it fulfilling. My current lifestyle isn't a complete reflection of who I am or who I want to be – work in progress, I suppose.

One thing that has been missing is this, writing. I'm not entirely sure what to write about, but maybe I'll start with all the things I couldn't say.

Surviving

There are No Words

Some things you just can't speak about.
Final breaths from a wet nose on a furry face,
all the doubt in the choices you've made;
holding wrinkled hands for the last time,
and that phone call to your aunt when you said goodbye.
The horrors you've put yourself through for years
and the true depth of your greatest fears –
that time the world for a moment went black
and how you were afraid you wouldn't come back.
The ache of infertility that hits in unexpected ways.
Wondering: *is this all I'll ever be for the rest of my days?*

Trauma

The crack in the porcelain that was never meant to be
slowly fissured out until it fractured the entire thing:
this is how I see the trauma in me.

It's a part of me now, though I wish it was not –
I hate how it taints every joyous thought.
I'm perpetually waiting for the next shoe to drop
and I'm unsure how to get this doom-filled thinking to stop.

Believe me, I don't like feeling this way
but it's like my vitality has left on holiday.
It's even hard to get some sleep
because my anxiety follows me into my dreams.

It feels impossible to take a deep breath
and I rarely stop moving until my body demands rest.
I do all the "right" things, hoping to get better soon
but oh – I want nothing more than to just be through,

through the processing, and move on with my life,
Living vibrantly, full of light –
but for now I carry this weight ever-present,
and the cracks in the porcelain just keep on spreading.

Panic Attacks

I can't breathe
Inhale, exhale
I can't speak
Gasping for air
My heart races
I'm going to die
A calm voice says, "you survived before."
My panic replies, "but not this time!"

I can't breathe
Inhale, exhale
My thoughts a violent storm
A rapid flurry of lightning
One panicked thought bleeding into the next
Gripping anything that will steady me with all my might

I can't breathe
Inhale, exhale
"Yes, you can"
Inhale, 1, 2, 3, 4
Hold
Exhale, 1, 2, 3, 4
Repeat until the storm loses its hold
Breathe in, 1, 2, 3, 4 – and let go

PTSD

Post-Traumatic Stress Disorder was a phrase I thought was only reserved for people who endured indescribable hardship: war-heroes, assault survivors, witnesses to heinous crimes against humanity. I didn't think I qualified, that I hadn't suffered enough to justify that diagnosis, that what I faced really wasn't terrible enough for my mind to react this way. I felt like an imposter every time my heart would race, my hands would shake and I would break out in a clammy sweat. That I was committing fraud every time my brain would spiral and I forgot how to breathe. That I was acting like a nonsensical fool every time I had to coax myself away from the verge of a panic attack. What I endured was scary, but not worthy of the label *trauma*… I should be able to get over it, right?

Well, *should* is a very dangerous word. It is a wall we build between us and the healing we deserve. Like pain, trauma is inherently grey, it can't be measured, it can't be compared, it is simply felt. It will leave scars, visible or not. All that matters, all the justification we need to seek support is how it makes us feel. So if, like me, you feel like your experience doesn't justify the visceral response you experience in your body every time a trigger initiates a slideshow of horrors in your mind, please know no amount of pride or shame is worth your ongoing suffering, and that "should" does not belong in the vocabulary of trauma.

A Matter of Logic

If it was a matter of logic my body would know she is safe,
but she's been battling for years, months, and days.
I don't know how to tell her we don't have to fight anymore:
we are well enough, we can let go of the intangible wars.
We can breathe in, breathe out, be present and kind
instead of fearing our life is on the line.
We aren't little or ill-equipped anymore,
we are strong enough to lay down our sword.
My brain knows this – but my body? She does not.
She is waiting, fight-ready, for her world to fall apart.

When you Meet a Bully

When you meet a bully don't look them in the eye –
not out of fear or avoidance – but to see a lovelier sight.

When you meet a bully don't give them your precious time –
their hourly rate isn't worth a second of your life.

When you meet a bully don't give them your ear –
there are sweeter sounds than their unfounded mutterings to hear.

When you meet a bully don't waste your words –
the breath in your lungs is too valuable to go unheard.

When you meet a bully protect others and yourself
for the difference it could make, and be brave enough
    to ask for help.

When you meet a bully, do better than I did.
Don't suffer in silence, holding it all in.
There is no reason to be ashamed. I promise –
it's never your fault, kid.

An Education in Cowardice

To bully a child takes one hell of a coward –
especially when it's a teacher, someone with power.
You didn't mold my mental fortitude,
you only inflicted needless wounds.
How dare you? Who gave you the right?
You were supposed to nurture me, not snuff out my light.
Only the weakest souls prey on a child –
only the cruel, the brutal, the vile.
I will never name names (you know who you are),
you will get no recognition beyond the memories you mar,
but the next time you think about putting a kid down
know this: karma's a carousel. What goes around comes around.

It Was Abuse

It was never okay, what you did.
You made me so ashamed, I withdrew, I hid.
You called it educational, an awakening,
but you never asked my permission, you didn't say anything.

You did as you wished
and I was your petrified witness,
too mortified to speak, and you thought you had me –
when I learned you'd violated others, we couldn't let you go free.

Though our justice system is laughable when it comes to
    punishing vile men
within your victim's sphere of influence you'll never hurt a
    woman again.
Know this, you pathetic example of a man:
I will never blame myself for your horrendous sins again.

Men who Take

No one really prepares you for men who take:
those who feel entitled to parts of you you don't want
    to give away.
But they take and they take without collecting any blame
and somehow women are the ones left with the tarnished name.
They take our pride, take our health, take our names
    and our wealth,
take our identities, our security, till we wonder 'what's left of me?'
They take all that you have until you're convinced
    you are nothing –
but that's the big secret, my dear   it's you who is something.
And these men who take are afraid of your power,
they know their privileged abuse is in its final hour.
They're trying to keep us down with all their might
because when push comes to shove we will win this fight
and make this world a better place:
one that no longer applauds the men who take.

At Least

I hate the phrase *at least*…
I know you were really sick but *at least* you didn't die.
I understand the loss you're mourning, but *at least* you had
    them for a time.
I'm sorry you endured trauma, but hey, *at least* you survived.

At least robs us of empathy by replacing it with its counterfeit,
    sympathy,
cutting off the beautiful potential for vulnerability.
At least feels more like rejection than acceptance,
like your troubles aren't really troubles when they're in the past
    tense.
At least says in the grand scheme of life your pain
    doesn't matter,
all while that very thing has left you feeling broken, raw,
    and shattered…

So please don't meet my agony with the phrase *at least* –
despite your best intentions it does not provide relief.
If my darkest demons leave you speechless, that's alright;
I hope for your sake you can't empathize with my sleepless
    nights.

Because the truth is, I'm not really looking for you to say
 anything at all.
It's my experience, my pain, I'll choose when and how I fly
 after this fall.
All I want is a witness for my sorrows, to share I'm not okay.
When we're done and you go on your way
you'll say, "*at least* I listened"; the only *at least* I need you to say.

Resilient Little Thing

You stand in the middle of the storm, wind whipping your face, rain pelting your goosefleshed skin. Stoic and steadfast you remain, raging against the storm as it rages against you. The elements may be fierce but you are mighty too. The wind may howl but it has nothing on a cry of defiance like yours. Its force may batter your body but its strength can't hold a candle to the fire in your heart. The rain may pour and the lightning streak across the sky with a ferocity that shakes the very heavens. But it cannot compare to the fight in your soul. The storm will pass but you, resilient little thing, will endure. Storms be damned.

Feeling

Nothing and Everything

Sometimes I feel so much that I go numb. My heart cracks open under the weight of emotion. Inside is a black hole, a void in my chest, a hollowed chasm where my heart used to beat, where no pain or light seeps in. It's a fortress no assault can penetrate. Walls so fortified that nothing bad or good can get in. There, I simply am.

I keep telling myself to feel it all, to find my way back to the child I was, who was told she was too sensitive for this callous world. I want to hold her and whisper, "my darling girl, your feeling heart is your greatest strength. Be brave, be kind, and feel it all. Teach people to love, to be gentle with the parts of ourselves with claws and fangs. If we can be kind to ourselves, we can be kind to others."

So here I am trying to again feel everything while feeling nothing. To become a sensitive soul in an unfeeling world.

Strength in Feeling

"You're too sensitive". I'm not even sure what that means.
It's immeasurably brave to show your feelings,
it's cowardice to bottle everything inside.
It's marketed as strength but we all know that's a lie –
it's easy to hide, to numb, to forget.
It takes courage to emote, and courage to truthfully live.

Sleeve Full of Hearts

I used to wear my heart on my sleeve,
but fear taught me that's not a safe way to be.
The softness inside must be protected by thick plates:
humor, intelligence, and logic keep dangers at bay.
There is no safety in feelings; you must stamp them down
    to be brave.
Be ruthless and cunning, never let emotions get in the way.
How I wish I had seen these so-called truths for the lies
    they were,
that no matter the path, in this life you will experience hurt.
Be kind and true and know your worth.
For the bravest thing is to feel, to hope, to burn.

Disappearing

When I am wounded deeply I go numb.
I feel nothing, I am hollow,
my very essence drained out of me.
I let my pain spill into the void
along with myself until there is nothing left
and we both cease to exist.

Honestly

Sometimes honesty hurts, and I don't like hurting others.
I would rather ache keeping my pain in, than inflict it
    on another.
It's uncomfortable to tell people they've hurt you –
I've always written it down, it seems the safest thing to do.
I fumble over my words unable to articulate how I feel.
And then the following happens, I know the pattern well.
For the blundered conversation and my own feelings I end up
    at fault,
and regret speaking up at all. So, often I keep my thoughts
    to myself,
keeping people at a safe distance; it's better if they don't know
    me well.
I remain the gentle, quiet flower on life's proverbial wall,
and honestly – only my heart and these pages know it all.

Privilege & Pain

Sometimes I wonder if my experiences have been all that heavy. Perhaps I'm beginning to falter, no longer able suck it up and carry on. I am privileged, there is no doubt about that. There are people struggling to survive, to get their basic needs met, people who cannot freely express themselves without fearing for their lives. I have not faced that degree of adversity, however, what I can speak to is this:

Being bullied by peers for being tall, clumsy and uncool.
Being ridiculed by teachers for having a brain that works
    differently than what they're used to.
Developing an eating disorder by age 15, that went unaddressed
    because no one would describe me as too skinny.
Living with chronic pain starting at the age of 14; I was 31
    before a diagnosis became a part of my story.
Learning the lesson of grief at ages 5, 11, 15, and as an adult
    more times than I'd like to count.
Forever losing my ability to carry a child from a condition
    most can't pronounce.
Being finally diagnosed with ADHD at age 33.
Caring for my spouse while they battle some unnamed medical
    mystery.
The slow unraveling of everything that used to make sense.
And the anxiety of feeling like my whole life is hanging in
    suspense.

Medical trauma that broke me in more ways than one.
And the feeling of simply being done, while my sense of
    obligation keeps me holding on.

There is a lot I don't know, but there is one thing I do. Despite our experiencing different kinds of pain, the shared experience of it connects me to you. In a world that seems more divided each day, pain teaches us we're more similar than not. It's a sentiment universally understood transcending language, culture, or any barrier keeping us apart.

Gentle Human, Fierce Heart

I had a conversation with little me today. She yelled and cried and raged. She said, "how could you let them do that to us?! Why didn't you fight back? Why didn't you answer their hate?" She screamed until her lungs were raw, her body wracked with sorrowful sobs. Then, through anger's haze, she lifted her gaze, and asked a simple question: "why?" I reached out my hand and said, "I don't know, but you're right. It wasn't fair, and it wasn't our fault we didn't know how to fight. But will you tame our demons with me now and beat back the dark? And show the world what it means to be a gentle human with a fierce heart?"

Un-everything

I am unraveling my emotions
and untangling my anxiety.
I am unlearning all the ways I have hated myself
and unteaching my mind that it's weak to ask for help.
I am untelling all the lies I've believed about my body
and unbinding all the expectations others have placed on me.
I am unmaking the image of who I thought I had to be
    in this world
and undoing the damage of all the hurts I didn't deserve.

My hope is that if I can unweave all the pain
and unworthiness I've held in my chest
then I can exist in a place of ease, be at home in myself.
Because all this unbecoming creates room to fill
with undimmable joy and unshakeable peace,
uncompromising self-worth
and the unfaltering strength to simply be –
unflinching faith in what my body is capable of
and unrestricted striving for the life I want.
Room for unending compassion for the women I've been
and unfaltering hope that this isn't where my story ends.

Under Tension

I don't feel like myself. My body feels heavy, bones weary from carrying the weight of my lifetime, from the obligations of the generations that came before. Keeping up with my neighbors by obtaining wealth and beautiful things. Accruing success so my family will say they're proud of me. Should I just let myself fade away, or keep fighting and clawing day after day? There has to be more to my life than this… grinding out an existence that looks pretty on paper but is bad for the soul. Sacrificing myself in the pursuit of prosperity. That is the crux of things, the tension between my responsibilities and my dreams.

My Closet Floor

I lie on the closet floor when it all feels like too much,
when it's hard to breathe and my mind starts to rush.
I lie there and think about running away
but time after time I choose to stay —
I breathe in through my nose, out through my mouth,
fighting to grab hold of the fear and drown the doubt.

Deep Feeler

I hope you know how sacred and special you are,
that your ever-expanding empathetic heart is leaving its mark.
There are few who are open to all the good and pain of this life –
a noble cause for which only the strongest are able to fight.
Seeing things so clearly often makes you feel alone,
though your nurturing soul is the very definition of home.

Deep feeler, remember when you are exhausted from trying,
please care for yourself. You can't light up the world if
   you're dying.
It's not your job alone to sustain each connection –
those who refuse to meet you are missing out on true affection.
If you find people are unable to love you the same way,
please hold out for kindred souls – you'll find them one day.

Deep feeler, have courage, feel everything as completely as you do.
Know that there will be some who try to take advantage of you.
It is not your responsibility to save those who are lost.
Protect your precious heart, don't let it pay their cost.
Though you may see the smallest redeeming qualities in
   their face,
if they aren't willing to change let their empty promises ricochet.

Deep feeler, you could heal the world with your embrace.
Keep existing intentionally, delightfully at your own pace.
Be proud of your tender heart at the end of each day,
and keep living wholly – come what may.

Raging

Water

I am a soothing presence to quench your thirst.
(But never forget that I can also be ice, and ice burns.)

I Asked

I asked for help but it wasn't convenient for you –
I guess my burdens weren't as important as the nothing you
    had to do.
Somehow it's fitting, though, that it's you who said no –
who taught me that needing help is a weakness exposed.
I strived to be a portrait of independence, a heart carved
    from stone,
but I am mortal, I am flawed, housed in flesh and skin
    and bones.

I have worked so hard to unlearn the damage of your
    good intentions,
and I was proud of myself for asking for help for a split second,
but your rejection made me feel irresponsible and small,
like it was all my fault, like I deserved it all.

Your dismissal says more about you than it does about me.
It's not wrong to ask for help, everyone deserves to be seen.
So I'll keep on reaching out my hand (just maybe not to you)
because when I *do* ask for help I deserve someone who'll
    follow through.

Liar

I don't care if it was out of some false sense of protecting me:
   you lied.
You knew that I wouldn't agree, so you lied.
Every day for almost two months you lied
to my face, even when I asked why the pills were piling up, you
   lied,
and no half-hearted, obligatory apology is going to make it
   okay. You lied.
And you're only sorry that I'm upset, not because you lied.

Let them be

Let them show you their true selves through their inconsiderate
    actions.
Let them put your hopes last and their dreams first without
    consideration.
Let them neglect your relationship, instead of begging on your
    knees for more.
Let them play referee as if it's all about keeping score.
Let them stay complacent while you choose to grow;
let them live out their life thinking you'll never go.
And when you have seen all you need to see,
decide what you're going to do about it, and then let them be.

The Man

Did my being myself emasculate you?
Since we're being honest, how about you tell me the truth —
did me finally taking care of myself pour salt in some wound?
Or upend your twisted "traditional" worldview?
Treating me as less doesn't make you more —
the truth of the matter is it only makes you poor.
Poor as a man, poor in thought,
poor despite the accolades you sought,
poor in honor, poor in respect,
poor in ways you haven't realized yet.
You think you're the big man when you walk into a room,
but I've never known a man quite as small as you.

The How Matters

I overheard a conversation today. "Well, at least I fold the laundry!" he said. "And if she doesn't like how I do it then she can re-fold it". The tone carried the stench of superiority. Women should be grateful for the help, right? I keep seeing men "help" their partners, doing household tasks the easiest way possible or simply wrong. Then expecting A credit for C effort. THE HOW MATTERS! How you fold the laundry, how you load the dishwasher, how you store the groceries. It's not really about the task getting done, it's about being seen. And when you notice the how, people feel seen. Notice the *how* of the next household chore. If you see the details, you'll see the person between them.

Election Day

Do not ask me to hope,
for you're asking too much.
Ask me to be angry,
ask me to rage, to mourn, to weep,
from the numbness I can muster that up.
But today, do not ask me to hope,
because you ask too much.

Disaster

I don't know what it's like for my life to go up in flames,
for floods to wash my home away,
for a hurricane to leave only its shattered frame.
But I do know that nature isn't the one to blame.
It's the people that deny the existence of climate change.
While they play pretend we'll look for to those providing aid –
it's people who change the world, not leaders (only in name).

Land of the Afraid

I am afraid for this country every day, as freedom dies and
    chaos reigns,
afraid to see integrity, justice and empathy eroding away,
afraid of once-astute minds become dull with misguided hate,
afraid of a leader that panders to dictators and bullies
    the brave.
Who will throw the innocent in jail because they got in his way.
Who wouldn't blink to gain power at the cost of humanity.
As he dismantles checks and balances, why aren't we stopping
    this insanity?
A president was elected and he self-appointed himself king.
With mourning hearts, a fearful requiem we now sing.
For the land of the afraid
and the home of the enslaved.

A Part of the Problem

A lot of political decisions hurt my heart. Politics are not *for the people, by the people* when they benefit the 0.1% and marginalize the rest. We've lost the human factor in humanity, the true north on the compass of our compassion. What happened? I've watched the deterioration of consideration in my lifetime. And it's not solely politicians to blame. I ask us to reflect and remember a kinder world is made by the little things. Putting your shopping cart away in the store parking lot. Placing your dirty mug in the dishwasher at work. Holding the elevator for the person five seconds behind you. Holding space for conflicting opinions without having the final word. Letting a car over with their blinker on in traffic; waving to the one who let you in to say *I appreciate you being kind*; getting over one lane to give space to emergency service vehicles who truly have a need to go, go. Thanking the "invisible" workers that make your day easier. Giving the security guard or garage toll worker a simple smile and hello. Putting your trash in the trash can. Instead of being part of the problem, putting a little more thought into thoughtful, and a little more kindness in humankind.

Land of the Immigrant

America is a nation of immigrants, settlers who stole the land from its native people. Whether your lineage arrived two hundred years ago or two, we are all immigrants. So what I'm failing to understand is why people have such a hard time with immigrants? What criteria make you American? How many generations removed you are from landing on this soil? Or is it where you came from? Often it feels like it has to do more with the color of someone's skin, and the value of what's in their pocket.

Hundreds of thousands of people are trying to navigate our convoluted system lawfully, and they are being stolen from their citizenship appointments. People who are trying to do the right thing are being kidnapped by groups of plain clothed government agents like delinquent vigilantes. You can't tell me there is justice in that. If it was just the hand of the government wouldn't be hiding away like thieves in baseball caps and masks. Sneaking around to steal mothers from children in a school parking lots, taking minors off of playgrounds, and tearing families apart. If this was right, we wouldn't be hiding ourselves with shame.

Our nation runs because of immigrants, our nation exists because of immigrants, our Constitution exists because of immigrants. The Declaration of Independence was written by immigrants. Our clothes, our food, our infrastructure, our homes, our buildings, everything that creates our sense of comfort was made possible by migrant hands. Because guess what? Privileged Americans don't want to do the work that new arrivals do. You want our nation to crumble? Get rid of the immigrants. Some of the most honest, hardworking people, truly the embodiment of the American dream. Tear them away from the pursuit of that dream, and we create a living nightmare for everyone.

You can stay oblivious in your glass house, head in the sand, ignoring the world on fire. But it's already at your door, it's on your street, it's at the grocery store. No one is unaffected by this. And if you want to lie to yourself, good luck. Because every immigrant in this nation – whether we've been here for generations or days – we're all going to lose. So maybe stand for real justice. Make America the land of the immigrant, as it has been for hundreds of years.

Learning

Atlas

He was a man who bore the weight of the world. But what about his mother? She had to bear the weight of the universe to birth such a man. For every unfathomable feat of man, there is a woman who has given more.

Enough

I used to want to be enough for others, now I want it
    for myself;
so you can put your judgments, criticisms, and slurs back on
    the shelf.
My shopping cart is full with integrity, appreciation, and
    self-respect,
the cost of appeasing you is not worth the emotional debt.
Go ahead and rant, do your worst,
I hope you have the kind of day you deserve.

To Myself in the Beginning

I stood on the sidelines of my memory and watched them tear
    me to shreds with their eyes,
calling me different, making me ashamed of my size.
When they strode out I walked over to little me and said,
    "I'm sorry".
I grabbed my small hands and looked into my eyes
and said, "don't for one second believe in their lies.
I can't tell you why it's like this, I still don't comprehend
what it was about us they just couldn't stand,
but I can promise you this: it won't last forever.
In the future it will be so much better.
So let their words roll off you like water off a duck;
darling girl, they aren't worth the years you'll feel stuck.
There are people ahead that are well worth your time –
You won't believe the friends you will have, how much they'll
    make you smile.
Remember these words, guard them close to your heart.
You are enough as you are, not a project to start."

One Day

One day you'll *think* I'm enough as I am,
and then you'll *feel* it too.
One day you'll *believe* all you need is within you,
and then beyond all doubt *know* it's true.

Homebody

I want to feel at home in my body. She has cared for me, protecting me from myself and a treacherous world. Full of capitalists exploiting my insecurities for a profit, hell-bent on making me hate her. She is the house for my soul, no other form could do it better. Her health ebbs and flows with the affection I'm able to give her. I owe her my life, and it's high time I repay her. With tenderness, warmth and abundant grace. Because in the end it's just me and her for the rest of our days.

Change

They say the only constant in life is change, and I'm certain
    they're right,
but if change is inevitable why is it something we try so
    hard to fight?
We resist and we clench our fist to keep comfort within
    our grip,
stumbling over the inescapable till finally we slip
and fall into a new normal that we realize was for our good.
When change comes yet again, I hope we embrace her
    as we should.

The Beauty of Being too Much

You are *too* much.

Too much to stay in a mediocre relationship.
Too much to deserve minimal effort.
Too much to ask for scraps of affection.
Too much for them to expand enough to hold all that you are.
Too much to be indifferent to your overflowing heart.
Too much to not appreciate what they have
and what they're going by to lose,
by being too little to hold you.

Possibly More

I keep trying to find my way back to the person I was,
but all my efforts just aren't enough.
Instead of containing rough edges within a self that no
    longer fits,
maybe I embrace the new sharp angles and jagged bits.
Keeping the essences of the girls and women I was before,
and assemble them in to a version who is more.
More patient with herself and kind,
too radiant to hide her cascading light,
more grounded in her truth unafraid of life,
and vibrant in a way that you can't help but smile.
I don't think happiness means finding a way back to
    my old self,
that girl has loved, lost, and been through hell.
It's embracing who I've been and laying each evolution to rest,
thanking them for carrying me here and doing their best.
If you also find who you were doesn't fit the soul within anymore,
I hope you'll thank who you've been, and embrace that
    you're possibly more.

My Body

She cries at me to stop and I don't listen
She forces me to hold space and I resist it
She feels like my nemesis but in truth is my greatest friend
She will house my stubborn heart until the end

Duality

I used to think that feelings could only happen one at a time. Occasionally overlapping if they were similar enough. Sad–angry. Wonder–joy. These days, however, I live in constant duality. I am overjoyed that people I love are welcoming a second child, and simultaneously grieving that I will never experience the miracle of creating one. I love my partner and I am equally frustrated by his ambivalence. I am so proud of myself for digging up and working through my trauma, and concurrently ashamed of the experience I've hidden like some festering secret. I am polarized, in constant conflict. I've also never felt more whole. I don't have to be this OR that, I am this AND that.

Kind vs. Nice

They are not the same. Kindness is the result of experiencing the darkness and choosing not to perpetuate it. It's choosing not to inflict on others what you have endured. They say hurt people hurt people, and for some that's true. But hurt people can also heal people. What kind of hurt person will you be? Kindness is rooted in otherness. It is thoughtful, compassionate, strong, empathetic, deliberate, actionable. It costs nothing to be kind; you have already paid in pain. But it costs others dearly when you pay them in hurt.

Being nice is about being accommodating, pleasing, agreeable, timid so that people like you. Niceness is self-focused. Most of my life I wanted to be nice, catering to the whims of others to be accepted. Contorting myself into whatever version was palatable. I'm not a nice person anymore. I burn at injustice, I get angry at bullies, I fiercely protect the people I love, I have integrity, I am steadfast and unwavering. I have suffered, known pain, witnessed the darkness of this world, the hate. And I have made my choice, to unleash myself upon this world with kindness.

I am not nice, but I am kind.

Fighting

Fine

She says *I'm fine* with tears in her eyes,
her chin lifts up and you glimpse the defiance inside.
Internally she's crumbling but a stranger would never see,
her posture says *I've got this* and the world lets her be.
If her wounds were visible on the outside,
there would be no hiding all she's survived.
But her scars are in her heart and her mind,
her unmarred skin a pretty lie.
Lately, as soon one wound heals another's inflicted,
leaving no time to bolster her resilience.
Soul weary from holding on,
one slip and her composure will be gone.
She whispers "you're not allowed to fracture, hold it together."
Because you can't fall apart when you're everyone's tether.

The Monsters

When I was a little girl the bullies found me strange.
Behind the teacher's back they'd call me horrid names.
I was born with a generous spirit and a wildly wonderful mind,
a fiery heart whose vibrant, flaming hues burned bright.
But with every slight and slander my flame got smaller
and the effervescent spirit folded, her shine getting duller,
until hatred for my body snuffed that fledgling flame out –
I crumpled under the weight of judgement and the
    monsters pounced.
Claws honed by nightmares, despair dripping from
    venomous fangs,
sinewed bodies and pitch black eyes with malice in their gaze.
They screeched, "you will never be loved, you will never be liked,
you will never be satisfied, you will hate yourself all your life!"
For decades they swirled around me, feeding on my heart.
No wonder I became so frightened of the dark.
Time passed, I grew up, but the little girl remains,
wounded and crying tears of gold-flecked flames,
within her hollow tomb lying curled up in a ball,
surviving to hold off the monsters who desire it all.
I can't tell you when. I'm not sure what the catalyst was,
but in our thirties the little girl and I decided we'd had enough.
We began striking tinder, coaxing sparks to life,
protecting fragile embers with all our combined might,
and slowly the embers grew into delicate flames,
enough to push back the darkness clinging to our frame.

Now we've resorted warmth that comes from within,
our renewed light shining gently through our skin.
We aren't the kaleidoscope of wild flame that was,
but our healing and rekindling has only barely begun.

Dearest Fear

Why do you keep showing up, unwelcome, on a beautiful day,
right in the middle of all my fun and play?
Why do you insist on tinging hope with doubt,
trying to convince me I should sit this one out?
Why do you take excitement and turn it into anxiousness?
Do you gain pleasure from my restlessness?
Or does it spring from some twisted duty to protect?
God, how I wish you would just let me rest.
I am exhausted from your spontaneous visits
and the occasions when you decided to move in for a bit.
Do you really have nothing better to do
than to turn my mind into a proverbial zoo?
Full of creatures with fangs that snarl and prowl,
that feast on joy with a vicious howl…
If you're trying to shield me, I can do that on my own,
but you keep me weak behind walls of trepidation and stone.
Because you don't want me strong, you want me dependent,
you want to control me like an indentured servant –
but my name is Meghan, and I will not be afraid.
And I will not waste on you my minutes, my hours, my days.

Imagining the Worst

I recently heard that the biggest misuse of imagination is worry,
the negative contrast to dreaming, the anti-imagination.
I exhaust my creativity to paint worst-case scenarios,
mastering the skill to the level of paid-professional.

As a child I lived in a world of my own design,
castles with secret gardens and walls covered in vines.
But now instead of housing hope and wonder,
the castle battlements are braced for phantom foes.

What a tragic waste! My creativity has felt distant,
the magic dried up defending against the unknown. No wonder.
I'd much rather use it to bring me life,
rather than sucking the light right out of me.

The Cost

I am tired of being resilient when all I want is to be soft. I am
    asked to endure, to hold on, but I ask "at what cost?".

My delicate skin, becoming tougher
than aged leather by the demands
that I must grow a thicker one.

My flesh, to the ravenous appetite of society's beasts
and my own insecurities. Be smaller! Meeker! Less!
Even when I'm a withered skeleton
They'd pick the marrow from my bones to feed their hunger.

My bones that bear the weight of this world,
have held empires and lifetimes and generations of men
who give less than a thought to me and my sisters.

My heart, the bloody thing in my chest
that sustains life. Bleeding out
in fear of the pain it hasn't yet endured.

My mind, sharp, cunning, intuitive.
To a life of safe monotony, empowering the powerful.
Only known by a chosen few.

My soul. The one thing that is mine, to a world
undeserving of a thing so divine.

Remember Who You Are

When they leave you mangled and bruised,
remind them of how you endure.

When they try to control your body,
remind them they can never entrap your mind.

When they try to shove you down,
remind them how you always rise.

When they drag your name through the mud,
remind them your value is innate.

When they tell you to sit down and be quiet,
remind them with how much authority you speak.

When they tell you "you will never make it",
remind them just how tenacious you can be.

When they tell you "you are worthless",
remember who the fuck you are.

For Gore or Glory

What does it look like when a woman shatters,
when the container of their essence can't be pieced together?
Will a phoenix or a monster emerge from the wreckage?

Will she be a revered firebird of wild, crackling flame,
magnificent burning wings trailing embers of hope?
Or something of teeth, claws and membranous wings,
fearsome, breathing smoke and gluttonous with rage?

I suppose it's contingent on why she breaks.
But one thing is for certain, whether for gore or glory
she will be something formidable to behold.

Phoenix

She rose from the ashes of a fire built to destroy her,
and the pyre that was created to consume her refined her.
The heat from the flames made her stronger,
and she wears her smoldering scars like armor.
Fire may destroy, but ashes give life;
those with will and a malleable heart survive.
The molten remains are poured into a new form,
stronger, purer, more durable than before.
Don't play with fire, they say, *you'll get burned.*
But it's in the fire that life's truest lessons are learned.
To those who tried to break her into kindling she says,
"I am a woman, stronger than you think
and you don't want to fuck with me".

You Do Not Yield

When they come to claim your voice for speaking too loud,
you do not yield.
When they turn the war cry of womanhood into a song
    of lament,
you do not yield.
When they seek to control you because they fear your wild,
you do not yield.
When they plot to turn your sisters against you because of
    our might united,
you do not yield.
When they turn waking dreams into living nightmares,
you do not yield.
When they try to shackle and break you,
you turn your eyes to the sky,
whisper *I will not be afraid*
and you do not yield.

She Won't Go Quietly

She lurks in the darkest shadows, skeletal and frightening,
a beast of nightmares dwelling inside me.
Her sharp talons grasp my mind in moments of peace,
reminding me my soul is hers to keep.
Her teeth are razor-sharp for tearing into me,
venom leaking into wounds she inflicts when I get too happy.
You see she wants to consume me until she's what I become,
a shell of myself, miserable, with nothing an no one.

Before she was a part of me I despised, she was created to protect,
keeping me unnoticed by tormenters critiquing my every step.
She kept me safe with fear, and humble with self-doubt,
she told me every mean thing imaginable before it came from
    someone else's mouth.
Eventually the bullies were gone but her thirst for control was not,
fortified by my insecurities my body she sought.
Every time I'd look in the mirror she'd seek to carve me down
    to an acceptable size,
but my figure would not succumb to her effort, or the different
    means she tried.

I went from a willing bystander to knowing that hurting myself
    was wrong,
and every time she lost control I bolstered myself to become
    strong.

She is now starved, ravenous from the years I've blocked her out,
pacing, waiting patiently in her fortified cell.
She is cunning, conniving and occasionally she slips through,
wreaking havoc, inducing panic till I can't breathe and my
    lips are blue.
She won't go quietly, convinced that without her the cruel
    world will destroy us,
which makes sense she was born from fear, from pain, from
    hate and distrust.

While I thank my daemon for her service I doubt we'll part
    as friends,
she hurt me more than they ever did and her time is at an end.
I will banish her from every inky recess of my mind,
healing until she has nowhere to go, nowhere to hide.
With her death knell she'll give a final blood curdling shriek,
because my soul is mine, and no longer hers to keep.

The Weight of Unspoken Words

Decades of unexpressed words hang like shackles around
    my neck,
I thought I'd carry them all with me to my death.
Unspoken words have weight, and have been mine alone
    to bear
for no other reason than that I was scared to share –
scared that my truth would hurt others or expose my weakness.
For too long now I've been weighed down by my secrets.
I hope you and I learn from my mistakes and save ourselves
    some pain,
that we might freely share our truths, and all the things we
    couldn't say.

Opening

To be Seen

What does it feel like?
That first big breath after being underwater a second too long
Cold shocking your face after leaving a warm room
The feeling of your feet grounding to the earth
The warmth of a blanket fresh out of the dryer
A shaft of sunlight on a cloudy day
Like being alive

Dixie Girl

For eleven years now my heart has lived outside of my chest.
Kept safe in a vault of black fur, floppy ears, four legs and a tail.
My heart was forfeit as down-payment for the greatest love I've
    ever known
from the moment she crawled into my lap on my parents porch.
My constant when life was a dream, a nightmare or something
    in between.
Warm brown eyes with flecks of amber that see right
    through me.
My rock who will lie with me on the floor
when the world feels too heavy to get up,
make me laugh with her dinnertime dance,
or aggressive nose-boops when I've been serious for too long.
My girl who loves rolling in the grass.
My couch cuddler, with the worlds softest ears.
Each new grey hairs on her face, fills me with agony and
    gratitude.
All thanks belongs to her, my North Star. She is mine,
    I am hers.
For eleven years now my heart has lived outside of my chest.
Kept safe in a vault of black fur, floppy ears, four legs
    and a tail.

Rae Rae

She is:

      My floofy white cloud with a silver lining

      The young soul that keeps my old one trying

      A pink nose I can't help but boop

      Joy when my heart is full of gloom

      A curious, busy nose that won't stop sniffing

      My weighted blanket when the world gets hazy

      The bright spot in my shadow, and kitchen co-dancer

Where his pointed-eared absence left a question,

   she is the answer.

Thankless Things

To sculpt David, Michelangelo needed a chisel.
To paint a Starry Night, Van Gogh needed a brush.
To write *Romeo and Juliet*, Shakespeare needed a quill.
It's never the tools that receive the accolades.
But I find awe in such ordinary, thankless things.

To the Dogs that Come After

To the dogs that love us after loss,
thank you for being exactly what we need.
Thank you for wiggling your nose into our lives
before grief slammed the door shut.
Thank you for restoring tenderness to a heart turned tough.
For your patience as we reshape our lives around new
    muddy paws,
and learn to lean on someone new when we fall.
Thank you for filling the fractures with overwhelming love,
and bringing in rainbows of light, a reminder from above.
I'm not sure how it works.
But I know with absolute certainty it's true,
that the one who came before chose you.

To the Moon
(for my Belize family)

I dream of a world where the gentle thrive,
where the world rewards not the cruel but the kind,
where the generous get through the day unscathed
and it isn't power but peace that people crave.
Maybe we're too soft for a place so mean…
or maybe we're exactly what this world needs.

Birthdays

How wonderful that there is a day
to commemorate your arrival to this world?
A day to celebrate that you've made it however many years
through this chaotic, beautiful, wild mess we call life?

My favorite part is reminding people that I love them.
It's their day. Sure – they may share it
with thousands of other people.
But it is my honor to share life with them,
I want them to know I don't take it for granted.

Birthdays are an opportunity to let people know
they are remembered, that their existence matters,
that their presence makes a difference,
that their absence would be noticed.
But year after year it seems without some kind of social
    announcement
birthdays often get forgotten. And I find that rather tragic.
It's like significant dates don't exist until they are posted
for the digital world to witness. We all deserve better than that.
Real life happens outside of a screen, with the people you love.

Dog Person

I've been known to rearrange my life for their happiness
because without them my own would cease to exist.
I sleep on the edge of the bed just to have them next to me,
their cuddles and sloppy kisses the best remedy,
their toothy smiles and wagging tails making a bad day
    feel better,
and rain, sleet or snow sounds like the perfect time to
    walk together.
All my clothes lovingly adorned with hair,
and my car windows with perpetual nose-smears,
tell you a dog is loved here.
Slobbery hands after a game of fetch,
poop bags stashed in my jacket pockets and car dash.
Dinner served at 5:01 is intolerably late.
I've only lived here a year yet the vet knows my name.
Time is never wasted when it's spent outside.
I'll love them for always, and all their joy is mine.

Give Them Your Time

I had things I wanted to get done this evening.
But you rested your head on my lap
and my only desire was to be your pillow.
Your paw claimed my arm which is now captive against
    your chest
my palm pressed up to feel your beating heart.
We've been sitting here for hours now.
It's time to go to bed, but I have no desire to move.
There will forever be a list of things to do,
but I won't always have you.

For B.

I hear the familiar pitter patter of paws in the sand,
you lay down beside me, sigh and then nose at my hand.
As if to say, don't be sad mom it will be alright,
as if cancer hadn't come like a thief for you in the night.
You look at me then, wise eyes saying *life will carry on,*
but for me every second will be an eternity with you gone.
You lick my cheek, trying to kiss my salty worries away.
You are my home, the one place I'm most safe.
You don't know what selfish is because selfless is all you know
     how to be,
I'd selfishly give every heartbeat, every breath to keep
     you with me.
You've marked me and made me who I am with each beat of
     your heart,
though life may try, not even death will tear us apart.
We are sealed, melded, forever intertwined,
God knew what he was doing when your life met mine.
The best parts of me are because of you,
you changed my world and you're not through.
I will cherish every minute we have, every fleeting second.
Remember you were mine first, the world's second.
While I needed you most, the world also needed your truth,
so everyone could learn that mice are mighty too.

A Gift

Every year over ten with a big dog is a gift
Every grey hair and milky-eyed gaze
Every tail wag and walk at a meandering pace
Every sniff and cuddle and ear perk when I say your name
Every sigh and grumble you make when dinner is late
Every roll in the grass to celebrate life in your wiggly way
Every second you're mine I will covet to the end of my days
Because you are mine, mine to me, forever and aways
And a piece of my soul is bound to yours through time and space
For more time with you I will eternally wish for one more day

My Words

Will my writing mean anything to those who read it? That's not really the point. It means something to me. It's my broken, bleeding, beautiful heart on a page, brave enough to be seen. It's intimately sharing facets of my existence, hoping that when light hits its edge it casts rainbows for others to cling to like radiant life rafts. It's the lullaby I sing myself in comfort, in gratitude for this terrifyingly precious life. It's being seen when I've been hidden for so long. It's claiming my place and making room so others can claim theirs too. It's my refuge, my solace, my home. My writing is me, and what a fiercely incredible thing that is.

Hurting

I Thought He Would Change

And for a while he did
until he got comfortable in his habits again –
I'm no longer motivation enough.
Does that says more about me, or him?

No

No is not a conversation, it's a two-letter word.
How can you reject my ideas before they are fully heard?
No is a full stop, shutting down my dreams and creativity.
No gives birth to *why should I try if they refuse to hear me?*

If I push back on your *no* in hope of a conversation
but you push it under the rug, shut down and walk away,
know my answer will be *no* when you face me in confusion
and ask me the question, "is everything okay?"

Silence Is an Answer

Doing nothing is still something.
I bared my truth, gave you time to think it through —
then a week went by, then two, then three.
I said, "hey, let's talk about it…" you said nothing.
I question whether you have thought about it at all.
Two days ago, I told you that silence is still an answer,
and not a good one, and you have a week before I'm done.
You said "there just hasn't been a good time",
and started playing another video game.
The pattern repeats, and I question why I stay.

Pretty Words

Pretty words won't give us a clean start
Pretty words won't heal a shattered heart
Pretty words won't fix inaction
Pretty words are just a distraction

Pretty words won't soothe persistent wounds
Pretty words won't make me forgive anytime soon
Pretty words won't make me forget
Pretty words do nothing for what's already dead

Pretty words won't bring us back to life
Pretty words won't make it suddenly alright
Pretty words won't restore confidence
Pretty words are just empty promises

Worth Fighting For

We had an argument, hours ago
and you didn't follow me from our bedroom.
I've been sitting in the dark alone,
waiting on the couch with a pen in my hand.
I've written three pages while you've
brushed your teeth and gone to bed.

Three pages of how I wish you'd fight for us,
instead of embracing a passive silence.
Tomorrow when we wake-up,
it will be as though tonight never happened.
This bitter truth chafes against my heart
and I can't bring myself to sleep next to you.

Because I can't forget that you left me alone,
I can hear you snoring while my tears fall.
I pull a blanket over my shoulders,
looking to any source for a shred of warmth.
While you dream I still wait
and brace for the dawn.

Morning Coffee

Used to be I didn't even have ask.
Now, you roll your eyes when I ask you,
like you have better things to do.
It's clear this nicety is a thing of the past.

So now I make my own every morning.
I question with each cup that is made,
like this small act of love, will we fade?
You no longer bring me coffee,
even when I wake yawning.

Time of Death

I'm trying to resuscitate something already dead:
throat raw from screaming, relentlessly pounding my fists into
   its chest.
I keep my lips on its lips, I can't admit that we're done,
though you're lifeless, cold, distant and frighteningly numb.
The monitor flatlines. The room falls silent.
A lawyer brings in the paper. All that's left is to sign it.

We Don't Talk

Something happened the other day. I immediately wanted to tell you, because of that one private joke we had, but we don't talk anymore. Not in a bad way, just the way the tides draw people apart. The way I see snippets of your life on my screen and I wonder how you are. The way I no longer know the details of your life, and that's a little strange. In the way it would be weird if I reached out on a random Tuesday. I understand now as I've gotten older that not all friendships are forever. Like a book put down, unfinished, without closure. And while it's okay, it's a little sad too, because sometimes I wish I still talked to you.

The Parts You Hate

The arms you thought looked bad, and hid with sleeves
held me tight and always felt like the safest place to be,
have cocooned me in warmth my whole life —
I know no securer place even at thirty-five.

The hips you always thought were too wide
took us on wild adventures, exploring for miles,
filling my childhood with joy and wonder,
within forests entire realms were discovered.

The tummy you complained was never flat enough
held life and then filled it with so much love.
A sign of all the delicious food we enjoyed as a family,
our time around the table I wouldn't trade for anything.

I never saw you as a sum of your "undesirable" parts,
I just saw my amazing mom who's a work of art.

Mom

I think you're gorgeous, I have my whole life,
I never saw the flaws you saw, but now my eyes are plagued
    with the same sight.
I want to be angry with you, but I just feel sad,
if you were anything like me, I hate that you ever felt this bad.
Is this the curse of womanhood?
We can appreciate another's beauty while cursing our own?
Daughters think mothers are beautiful,
while mothers chase the shape of their youth.
And mother's think daughters are beautiful,
while daughters battle the self-hate modeled by you.
I wish you could see what I've seen my whole life,
A woman who doesn't know just how gloriously she shines.
I'm trying now, to see myself with kinder eyes,
I don't want to waste my life loathing my hips and thighs.
So dear mothers, present and future, please be kind to
    yourselves,
if not for you then for your daughters, so they can love
    themselves.

Please Don't Forget

What happens when you forget?
When our memories no longer live rent free in your head?
Will you remember that time you took us down to the beach?
You watched us climb all over dad and it was too cold to dip
    in our feet.
Will you remember the summers we road-tripped to visit family?
We listened to Harry Potter books on tape endlessly.

Will you remember when you taught us how to cook?
We would each pick recipes to prepare with you after school.
Or how it was you who taught me to create?
The Halloween game board, the beaded icicles, that anything
    I could dream I could make.

How about that time I took you to Wimberley?
I tripped in that hole and just like when I was a kid you took
    care of me.
We aren't there yet, but I'm so afraid of all the things you
    may forget.
Dreading the day that I alone have these memories living rent
    free in my head.

Asking

What to Do

Seeking wisdom from a friend over coffee
I told her my latest sorrows when it comes to you.
Admitting *I'm not sure he'd notice if I never came back,*
Which led me to wonder how you'd react if…

I said it was over what would you do?
Would you beg on your knees till they're black and blue?
Would you be at a loss? Would it seem out of the blue?
Or would you finally pick up on the years of clues?
Would you finally see me like I always wish you would?
Or would you even notice me when I walk out for good?

Solace over coffee is over so I hug my friend goodbye,
I get into my car, turn the key, while dying a little inside.
I'm torn apart by my questions, not knowing the answer,
but I turn my car towards home and pull myself together.

The Lost Boys

I hear my friends asking, where are all the men?
The ones never enthralled by Neverland?
A generation of lost boys who refuse to grow up,
heedless of the crocodile clock ticking towards their breakup.
Instead they arm themselves with wooden swords and avoidance,
fighting off a love that would be their deliverance.
Chanting Peter's anthem, *'you can't catch me and make me a man!'*
running from their problems, playing a life-long game of pretend.
Peter banished his emotions, swearing never to feel them,
it feels like every boy my age clings to the same ideal.
And just like Pan they lose their Wendy,
then audaciously cry *I would have changed if she had just helped me!*
Hear me now lost boys and listen well,
we can't help you, you have to save yourselves,
you can't freeze time and forever is an awfully long time
    to be alone,
and growing up might just be the biggest adventure of all.

When we First Met

I thought I was pretty good at loving myself
but since then I've found a deeper well,
and what felt like adoration
is now like barely surviving from day to day.

I've been asking you to listen, to hear me.
I'm working so hard at loving myself
that I'm beginning to spill over the edges
of you, my container.

All my effort to explain this is not enough.
I don't think it's healthy to beg for love.
I won't empty parts of myself to fit within you –
either expand enough to hold me or
I'll find a new container with more room.

Connection

I wish you would say something.
Despite my best efforts I can't read your mind
I ask you "is everything okay?" all the time.
I can see in your posture that something is off
but you say nothing is wrong.
You're quiet, aloof and disengaged.
I try to connect, but you pull away.

I feel defeated and unsure. At least I'm trying.
It's hard to strike a balance, and not feel like I'm prying.

I wish you would share what's on your mind,
what makes you ache, what makes you smile.
I care, I want to hear it all, and not converse alone.
Anything other than this quiet resistance, this haunting dial tone.

What to Do

Seeking wisdom from a friend over coffee
I told her my latest sorrows when it comes to you.
Admitting *I'm not sure he'd notice if I never came back,*
Which led me to wonder how you'd react if…

I said it was over what would you do?
Would you beg on your knees till they're black and blue?
Would you be at a loss? Would it seem out of the blue?
Or would you finally pick up on the years of clues?
Would you finally see me like I always wish you would?
Or would you even notice me when I walk out for good?

Solace over coffee is over so I hug my friend goodbye,
I get into my car, turn the key, while dying a little inside.
I'm torn apart by my questions, not knowing the answer,
but I turn my car towards home and pull myself together.

But do you?

You say *I love you more, I love you the most-est.*
And I believe that you believe that it's true,
but it's not my reality.
If you loved me in the way you believe that you do
then I wouldn't have to keep begging for change.
I wouldn't have to strain my eyes to glimpse your emotions
through the cracks in the walls you put up —
you would just tell me.
I wouldn't feel like I'm a stranger,
you would make the effort to understand me.
I wouldn't have to repeatedly, explicitly state my needs,
because you would see me.
My throat wouldn't be hoarse from asking,
because the first time I spoke you would have heard me.
I believe that you believe you love me more.
But I'm the one trying,
hopelessly, to get through to you.

All the Things I Said

Not all relationships end in violent burning ash and flame,
some die subtly, complacency eating affection away.
I could never stop loving you overnight,
but your lack of effort has chipped away my fight.
Maybe this slow withering is partially my fault too;
I became exhausted putting the effort in for two.

I reached out my hand and you turned it away,
and I gave up a little more each time you say:
it's not your thing, you don't want to spend the money,
you're too stressed, it's not fun to do x, y, z.
All I hear is my interests aren't worth your time,
my company not worth your dime,
that I am a burden
and at the cost of your convenience I'm not worth it.

You objectify me and call it love,
this counterfeit version of affection is not enough.
You've touched me in ways I've told you I don't like,
an intimate caress that makes my body clench for a fight.
Yet you're the one who's offended when I hold you at bay,
though you're the one disrespecting my cues, eating my
    trust away,
as if you know what I like better than me.
Can you not see how that ignorance stings?

I don't want a child with you anymore.
It's led to more than one night of crying on the floor.
How can I raise them when I feel like I'm raising you?
Our kids deserve not one struggling parent, but a present two.

When I married you I thought I was getting a partner,
but rather than draw us close the years are pushing us
    apart farther.
I fight tooth and nail to get you to talk to me –
after six years and half a million hours shouldn't it be easy?
When I wanted to go back to therapy I met silence and excuses.
Is our marriage not worth the time, money, and effort
    you're refusing?
You try to placate me with pretty words: smart, beautiful,
    kind, funny.
After all this time, are these the best adjectives you have for me?

I survive on the breadcrumbs of effort you feed me,
why I don't get the version you are with friends and family?
Each time we talk I hope the change will stick,
but I only become increasingly malnourished, starving and sick.
You're a good man, of that I have no doubt,
but are we still good for each other? I can't say for sure now.
Soon I'll have to decide: a lifetime with you at the cost of me,
or do I start over, alone but set free?

If I could I would

How do you make a man see
that you're worn to the bone
that you're drowning under the mental load
that you work a six-figure job
then come home to work a second job that is not?

Make him see that your efforts set the stage for the week's success,
that it hurts that he's unsatisfied when you're doing your best.
See that having to mother him is not a catalyst for sex
(then he pouts like a child if you don't get undressed).

Make him see that you're succumbing to the weight of it all.
That when it comes to your relationship he's dropping the ball.
That his ambivalence is pushing you to the brink,
and how much it hurts when he "just didn't think" –
they say you can't make a thoughtless man thoughtful.
Waiting for him to change makes you look like a fool.

He asks for you to help him, to tell him what to do,
but you can't make him see. If you could then you would.

Indifferent

My love is slowly turning to indifference.
I don't think you realize how dangerous that is,
when someone who feels so deeply starts to feel nothing.
The very thought should be utterly terrifying.
I've been giving my all and I'm exhausted from trying;
my emotions towards you are withering and dying,
a slow death of real love and connection.
I wish my silence would spur you to action.
I feel really bad for you, truly I do –
you've *really* fucked up if I'm indifferent to you.

Not at that Cost

I want what is best for you, but not at the cost of myself.
I refuse to let what started so good turn into a living hell.
I've changed so much, become the most honest version of me
    I've ever been,
while you've stayed steadily comfortable, no real desire to
    grow within.
I'll give everything I have to sustain the remnants of us, but
if I could feel the fight in you, we could rebuild some trust.
I believed love was worth sacrificing everything,
with every fiber and cell,
but no longer at the cost of myself.

Are you sad too?

Our relationship makes me sad more than it makes me happy.
Am I alone in this too? Or do you feel the same about me?
Do you keep these thoughts to yourself, assume it will get better,
hope that happy memories will be enough to keep us together?
I don't have the answers – I can barely wrap my head around
     this mess.
But I know I don't want to spend our forever being sad like this.

What I Want

For you to hear me when I talk
For you to not shut down and put up walls
For you to not go to sleep while I'm still awake crying
For you meet my effort because I'm trying
For you to leave a lamp on so I don't come home to the lights out
For you to let me know when you're coming back to our house
For you to say goodnight before crawling into bed without me
For you to do things you might not like for the sake of my
    company
For you to encourage me to be my own person
For you to try because I'm worth it
For you to not be threatened by my independence
For you to not make me compete with a screen for your attention
For you to support me without expecting to be praised
For you to help me plan our dogs' birthdays
For you to listen to me and action it
For date night to be a privilege and not a box to check
For you to approach with curiosity and not judgement
For you to pursue the growth on the other side of discomfort
For you to never lose interest in getting to know me
For you to want to make my coffee on Sunday mornings
For you to buy me flowers just because it'll make me smile
For you to fight with me because figuring us out is worthwhile
For you to tell me how you feel
For you to help me, help us heal

Loving

Love is a Choice

Loving you is like the first sip of a really good cup of coffee, bringing warmth to the deepest parts of me.

Loving you is a hug after a long day at work, exhausted and leaning into your support.

Loving you is having a theme song for all of our adventures.

Loving you is arguing over who the dogs love more (even though we both know it's me).

In loving you, I'm the current bringing life to your calm waters, and you're the banks to my river.

Loving you is growth: we challenge each other, balance each other, fall and rise together.

Loving you is weekend nature walks, saying *hey! Come check out this sunset*, and narrating our dog's thoughts.

Loving you is knowing you'll wear a Hawaiian shirt on Thursdays. You become an expert in your hobbies and lemon-anything is your favorite dessert.

Loving you is a choice I make today and every day.

What Is Happiness?

A cool breeze on a warm afternoon
Tails wagging when you open the door
A quiet walk through the trees
Seeing hard work come to fruition
A loved one remembering how you like your coffee
Connecting with a friend you haven't seen in a while
A long hug after an even longer day
Being seen as you are – and loved deeply

Slow it Down

Slow it down, so I can find joy in the dimple of your smile
Slow it down, so we can stay here a while
Slow it down, so I can delight in the way our hands fit together
Slow it down, so we can stay in this moment forever
Slow it down, so I can luxuriate in the way our bodies intertwine
Slow it down, and say you'll always be mine
Slow it down, so I can marvel at the space between your breaths
Slow it down, so I can wonder at the rise and fall of your chest
Slow it down, I beg you, make each second last forever
Slow it down, because all we're guaranteed is this one
    moment together

To Know Love

You know how sometimes you meet a soul and you know that loving them will wreck you? Good or bad, build or destroy, you will never be the same, irrevocably different. But you do it anyway, because the turmoil and heartache are worth the risk. That joy and elation. To be known and seen. It's why we come back to love over and over again. Why we keep trying on the chance that we find a love that sticks, a love that's true, a love that grows with us. Because for however long or brief, our weary, life-worn souls find a home.

Beloved

I sigh, eyes to the sky, and whisper to the clouds above…
all I ever wanted was to be beloved,
not for what I could do, but for who I was.

Selfish

I will beg, steal and gamble for another moment with you. There is no being I love more than you and the cost of loving you will be the loss of myself. Your possession of my heart irrevocable and absolute. I would pay over and over again for the years we've had together. For my soul will seek yours in every lifetime in any form. I will indulge in nothing less than eternity with you. You are mine, I am yours, for evermore.

With Every Breath

I love you.
Like lungs exist to take in air.
Like the stars come to life in the night.
With all the innocent wonder of a child
and the knowing that comes with forty years of studying
    your smile.
I love you, and will love you, with every breath your mine.

The Women Who Have Healed Me

The women I know, love and call my friends
have stitched the rough edges of my heart back together again.
Whether we see each other often, or hardly at all
their presence in my life is a healing balm,
their names embroidered on every stich and seam –
it's because of them I know what true friendship means.
Sisters in soul, always close to my patchwork heart:
one thread at a time, you've turned it into a piece of art.

Sisterhood

You don't have to have to be born with one to feel it.
It's in the long hugs at the airport saying hello and goodbye,
the late-night text making sure you got home alright.
It's cheering each other's feats as you reach beyond the sky,
and in knowing they'll catch you if you fall no matter how
    high you fly.
It's in the small moments, and in the ones where you really
    want to quit.
It's in the *This made me think of you*, or the *Have you been getting*
    enough sleep?
It's in showing up, regardless of the miles and the time zones
    in between,
it's in the shared jokes, the secret looks and anticipating a need,
it's in *I've got your back*, it's in *Let me hold you while you cry.*
It's in every *Come as you are, for us you don't need to try.*
It's sitting on the floor with you, helping you up to try again.
It's something much more dear than the title of best friend.
It's knowing that the greatest loves of your life aren't just a
    woman or a man,
but the sisters that will hold you and carry you till the very end.

When Places and People Collide

When my dear friend moved to Scotland, the home of my soul, I thought I would be jealous to no end. But I'm not, not in the slightest. I am filled with unending warmth. I get to watch her fall in love with the place that has captivated me since I was three, learning to make daisy chains in our elderly neighbor's yard.

Scotland is wild and wonderful.

The sound of bagpipes, the ancient stone buildings, the rugged coast of the North Sea. The vibrant people and expansive moors, the smell of heather on the breeze, the untamed peaks, the mystical fairy pools, the primordial forests and fathomless lochs.

I long for the bite of fresh Scottish air on my face, but a little piece of my soul is soothed knowing the sister of my heart is there.

When the places and people you love collide there is space for immeasurable joy, if you allow it.

A new thing to share with them, a new layer of you revealed to them.

And some time in the future, when you're trying to describe the magic of this place to people who don't comprehend, you'll share a look with your friend and know you are understood.

Dear Stranger,

I love you. No conditions, no expectations, no action required. You, as you are right now, are enough. Read that again. You are never too much and you are always enough.

I want you to know love can come from the most unlikely places, and it should come freely – it doesn't need to be earned, it need have no strings attached.

Love can come in many forms, a smile from a fellow morning commuter, the embrace of a friend, the tail-wag of a dog, or a coworker who brings you an afternoon coffee.

The beautiful thing about love is it can't be confined to a box, no matter what society tries to tell us about what love is right or wrong. Love just is. Give love freely and in abundance, not only to others but also to yourself. Love yourself wildly and with abandon because, damn it, you deserve it.

With all my love.

Grieving

I'm Sorry for Your Loss

What I really mean is I'm sorry your heart is now acquainted with the kind of grief mine knows so intimately. I'm sorry for the aching void in the cavity formerly known as your heart. I'm sorry you have become familiar with this kind of pain that far too many and somehow, far too few know.

Only those of us who have loved and been loved in equal measure have the privilege of living with this type of scar. I'm not sorry that you have known this kind of love, in fact I consider you lucky for it.

I am deeply sorry that this love has been lost to you, separated from you by the distance between the living and the dead. Far enough that warmth and reassurance is only felt in the smallest reminders. Like a rainbow in a foreboding sky.

I'm sorry for the loss of a love so real that even when your bones are an echo of dust in the dirt it will still live on. Because a love like that can never truly be gone.

Fragile

What would you say if I said life is fragile?
Would you say, "I know, I know…"
or would you look at me with somber eyes that speak
    of knowing?
Would your shoulders cave in slightly, protecting that tender
    spot in your chest?
Would your lips press together to hold back a name?
Would you exhale the intangible heaviness surrounding
    your heart?
Would your mind travel back to a place and moment in time?
Or would you say, with quiet understanding, "yes, yes, I know"?

Eulogy

It's difficult to summarize a life into a few words.
To condense its impact to one speech.
It's even more difficult to articulate the depth of sorrow felt.

Madison's Poem

The death of a massive star results in one of two things:
a depthless void or a new, light-filled being.
How kind or cruel for the universe
to give us such an astute parallel for loss.
Loving luminous hearts come with a cost.

From a supernova a newborn neutron star can be made
like hope in the midst of pain.
But when grief's gravity causes a supernova to collapse,
it creates a black hole, a force no light can surpass.

If grief is love with nowhere to go
then my grief in your death is a supermassive black hole.
My sorrow a vortex so dark it absorbs all light,
hope and healing seem like an impossible fight.

The tale of Medusa an Perseus contains new meaning,
 their constellation holding your story eternally.
Just like the combustion of stars in the galaxy,
love and loss leave their mark on us irrevocably.

Grief that Whispers

Some grief doesn't scream, it whispers.
    A longing that was never fulfilled,
    a dream never realized.
    A loss that was for the best,
    an end that was healthy,
    a break that was a beginning.
    A death that was buried years ago.
    A string of unmet expectations,
    or painful self-fulfilling prophecies.
    Realizing you aren't where you thought you'd be,
    and wondering how you got here.
Some grief doesn't scream, it whispers,
and the quiet is deafening.

Always too Early

Why is it that death always arrives too early? Even the slow goodbyes feel jarring to the heart. Of death people say they were taken from us too soon, we never saw it coming, or we weren't ready… as if we ever are.

I honestly wish death wasn't so prompt, like a horse bolting through the gate. I'd rather it were like that endearing friend you can always rely on to be late, leisurely arriving after peace has been made.

Death can be traumatic and sudden, or suffering and slow. But either way loved ones are never ready for the dying to go.

Perhaps the living aren't meant to understand death's timing and it will always seem too early to those of us left behind.

Maybe for the dying death arrives with a warm embrace, like that punctual friend who always arrives exactly on time.

Love of My Life

I will never be ready for the day her warm brown eyes leave me,
but I can feel it coming, lurking in the shadows waiting.
Every unexpected vet appointment it reveals itself a little more,
a waking nightmare given flesh and form.
I've never been so afraid of anything in my life,
the fear of it resulting in more than one sleepless night.
It seeks to take away the soul I love most,
brown eyes that for over a decade have been my home.

Without You

My heart stopped beating when yours did.
That version of me that shared time and space with you ceased
to exist when your soul left your body. She couldn't bear
to exist in a home without the excited tap of your paws and
the sight of your frosted face after a long day. She couldn't sleep
without you chasing rabbits in your dreams beside her.
    She forget how
to breathe without your head in her lap grounding her.
    She couldn't bear
the weight of a life without you, and refused to be separated
    from you.
And so she hid her soul in yours with your final breath,
so all that's left is her earthly body and a hollow chest.

For the Forgotten

When I see them on the side of the road, the furry souls others
    forgot,
I whisper I'm sorry, and claim them because someone else
    did not.
I tell each of them you deserved so much more,
I'm so sorry a gentle soul didn't find you before.
I invite each one to dwell with me on the other side of eternity,
where they will be showered with love, if they can wait for me.
When I get to heaven and I open my door,
it will be filled to the brim with wet noses and hair covered
    floors.
Even though in this life they didn't have the love they deserved,
they'll never know a moment without it in haven as far as
    I'm concerned.

Losing You

This year my heart has died a thousand times.

It's been trampled, thrown about and smashed
into a million pieces – but it still keeps beating.

I keep wondering what it is that will do it in, the thing
from which it won't be able to recover.

The answer? Losing you.

Stay

I hold you tight, afraid to let go.
Thinking of all the things that only you know.
My mind whispers stay, I hold a little tighter.
    stay
You can let go now. You've been such a fighter.
    stay
I promise we won't let the stitches
you've sewn into this family fall apart.
    stay
Thank you for loving us so wholly
with all your heart.
    stay
Everyone we love on the other side is waiting for you.
    stay
Run wild and free. I know a piece of you
will always be with me.
    stay
I tell you every good and gentle and reassuring thing I can
    think to say
Except the one thing I most want to.
    Stay.

Crawling

It Ends with Me

Repressing feelings until all I know is numbness,
it ends with me.
This placating disposition catering to those who don't deserve her,
it ends with me.
Abandoning myself in the pursuit of material success,
it ends with me.
Absence to earn a dollar, a dime, an accolade for my pride,
it ends with me.
Manipulating my body to meet standards that weren't set by me,
it ends with me.
This pervasive anxiety, this bitter ambition, this crippling
    inadequacy,
it ends with me.
I will not pass these afflictions on for another generation to bear,
unyielding in the pursuit of healing, it *will* end with me.

2025.04.18

In my therapists office, on April 18th, my life changed
I stepped out of old patterns and into a new phase.
My inner child begged for me to let the darkness go,
I never knew it was my white-knuckle grip tethering its hold.
She put her hand on top of mine as I let the black veil slip
out of my grasp and into the night sky it went.
As it drifted away out of sight
my breath was taken away by the most vibrant sky.
A night sky full of stars, a sky for the dreamers,
a sky filled with hope and my endless wonder.
My inner child said "this is where all you magic lives,
look at all the light our sorrow hid".
I said, "what if it comes back?" She replied, "it won't ever again
the darkness is gone now it's time to let the light in.
The hardest part is over now, you did what we never could"
She pointed over my shoulder and there every version of me stood
She said, "we weren't strong enough to fight,
but we knew you would be able to bring back the light".
I stood and we all embraced as one,
every version melding into me because the fight was won.
Little me gave me one last hug goodbye,
then I was alone surrounded by the magnificent night sky.
Now I'm sitting here writing this, trying to get it all down,
because my life has changed, and I never want to forget the how.

Lessons From Books

Hope can feel illusive in the face of adversity,
leaving you suffocated by the weight of this world.
So I remind myself…
    I will not be afraid.
    You do not yield.
    Have courage and be kind.
Because even when the darkness engulfs me,
hope can blaze again, and banish the dark.
Even from the tiniest spark.

Child-Shaped Void

I cry when people are nice to me,
or anytime someone makes me feel seen.
I'm not entirely sure why
or what it means
except it fills a child-shaped void in me.

Choose Yourself

To the kids that were picked last in gym, skipped over as if invisible. To the perpetual wallflowers, and the ones that were never asked to be someone's date for the dance. To the ones that never received a prom-posal, or had their crush return their smile. To the brave who faced disappointed eyes when meeting their online date. And the ones who witnessed their friends fall over and over again while waiting for their first. To the ones whose birthdays and milestones go unmarked. And the ones who exercise grace like it's an Olympic sport. To everyone and anyone who has been picked last, or not at all. If you've never been chosen first, I hope, with all my heart, you learn to choose yourself.

Ordinary Days (Are Underrated)

This morning as I was making my coffee
I ran through my to-do list. Though I might lament it,
future me will thank me for it. What a privilege it is
to wage this battle on ordinary days!
The luxury of choice, the gift of time, the peace of ease.

Society suggests that unless your life is extraordinary
you are insignificant. Honestly,
I've always found the grind to do something and be
    someone exhausting.
And who is it for, anyway? Certainly not for me.
But for the societal belief that I ought to want,
that I should desire to aspire to more.

To my people, to the people who matter, I already am someone.
What I am doing does matter in my little sphere of influence,
and that is enough. So yes, most days in my life are ordinary.

But how extraordinary is that, in a world constantly trying
    to be more?
Me and my ordinary days are extraordinarily enough.

Some Days

Mondays I want to know what it feels like to be soft,
to lay down my sword and shed the weight of my armor.

Tuesdays I want to know what it feels like to be cared for,
to have my needs anticipated instead of shouted and yet
    ignored.

Wednesdays I want to know what it feels like to be at peace,
to have the space for quiet and stillness in my chaotic mind.

Thursdays I want to know what it feels like to be cherished,
to be celebrated for merely existing, and to revel in the love
    of it all.

Fridays I want to know what it feels like to be alive,
to have every cell in my body wake with effervescent joy.

Saturdays I want to know what it feels like to be untethered,
to amble through the wild without responsibilities or fears.

Sundays I wish to feel each of these things every day,
to embrace the thrill of being known, seen, loved and fully
    present.

No Longer Fit

Sometimes an old friendship becomes uncomfortable, like an old beloved pair of shoes that just don't fit right anymore. You've outgrown who you were when you first met them, but they can't seem to embrace all that you are now. There is no bad blood, no harsh words exchanged, but the familiarity is gone. Wearing them for a while is tiring, rubs you raw. For sentimentality they remain in your closet, but they are no longer your default. Maybe one day the stiffness will ease from your soles and you'll find comfort in each other's familiarity, but if not it's alright. Someone else's comfort isn't worth your stagnation. Forever friends will grow alongside you, getting more comfortable with each wear - like that one threadbare sweatshirt that fits perfect every time.

Muir Woods

Alone in the woods I feel like myself
instead of some frightened unfamiliar thing.
I breathe in the mossy stillness.
Though the world may rage and rattle,
I come home to the woods and am restored.

To Be a Bird

I wish I could fly somewhere new anytime conditions turn unfavorable. Soaring place to place, sheltering but never building a nest. I'd return to my favorite cities after storms cleared and enjoy the sun. The very definition of a fair-weather friend, careless and free. But the trappings of my human life keep me tethered, and the beings I love too much to leave keep me grounded. Some days, like today, I wish I was a bird. And tonight, when I am surrounded by the hearts I love, I'll be grateful for a nest to return home to.

Closing Thoughts

Caterpillars are rarely praised for what they endure to become the beauty we behold in their butterfly form. I feel like we often think of ourselves in the same way when we're in the process of evolving. Instead of appreciating our ability to endure, we become focused on where we wish to be, missing out on the process of becoming. This book is an ode to that process.

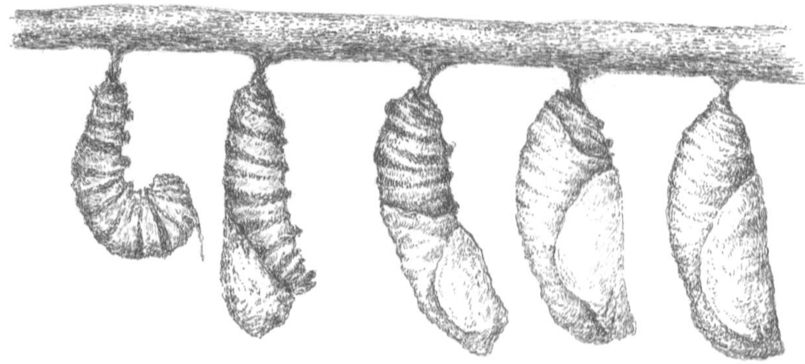

The Caterpillar

I crawled across parched land where my past selves were
   laid waste,
up mountains with endless false peaks seeking the façade
   of perfection.
I inched through canyons carved from the perilous river
   of expectation,
through plains of grass that whispered of all the ways
   I had failed.

I crawled until the waters overwhelmed me, the jagged terrain
   became too steep,
the winds of insufficiency a roaring sound, and my soul
   parched for self.
So I withdrew into the silence and safety of my cocoon,
to find myself, to find my peace.

Acknowledgements

To you, dear reader, thank you. I am forever grateful that you chose to pick-up my book and share your precious time with my words. I cannot thank you enough for your presence and trust.

To my beloved friends Colleen, Rachael, Leah, Ally, Jess, Lexi, Lynn and my therapists (you know who you are) thank you for being my safe space to share my writing for the first time. It would have taken me much longer to muster the courage to publish this book without you.

To my husband, this book changed us both in many ways. Thank you for seeing it as an opportunity to grow together.

To my family and friends who encouraged me along the way, thank you for your support. I will cherish it forever.

To every creative who helped me turn my manuscript into a real book, thank you for your guidance, mentorship and artistry. You have each honed your craft and it is my privilege to have worked with you. Thanks to Martha Sprackland for your editorial help. Thank you Iulia Mirica for your amazing artistry. Lastly, thanks to Victoria Heath Silk for the beautiful cover design and interior formatting.

About the Author

Meghan entered this world as a gentle human, and then developed a fierce heart through her own experiences and observing the world. Throughout her life she has instinctually turned to books and writing as a refuge and a place to make sense of her thoughts. Meghan was raised globally with ties to Texas, where she now lives with her husband and two dogs (Dixie and Rae).